Easy Lenny Lazmon
and the
Great Western
Ascension

Easy Lenny Lazmon and the Great Western Ascension

by Anton Piatigorsky

Playwrights Canada Press
Toronto•Canada

Easy Lenny Lazmon and the Great Western Ascension ©
Copyright 2000 Anton Piatigorsky

Playwrights Canada Press
54 Wolseley Street, 2nd Floor
Toronto, Ontario CANADA M5T 1A5
(416) 703-0201 fax (416) 703-0059
info@puc.ca   www.puc.ca

Playwrights Canada Press acknowledges the support of
The Canada Council for the Arts for our publishing programme and
the Ontario Arts Council.

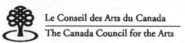

Le Conseil des Arts du Canada
The Canada Council for the Arts

ONTARIO ARTS
COUNCIL

CONSEIL DES ARTS
DE L'ONTARIO

Cover design: SirenmediA
Actor: Alon Nashman

Canadian Cataloguing in Publication Data

Piatigorsky, Anton, 1972-
    Easy Lenny Lazmon and the great western ascension

A play.
ISBN 0-88754-588-2

I. Title

PS8581.I218E27 2000   C812'.6   C00-930011-2
PR9199.3.P479E27 2000

First edition: July 2000
Printed and bound by Hignell Printing at Winnipeg, Manitoba, Canada.

Anton Piatigorsky studied religion and theatre at Brown University. His plays include: *The Kabbalistic Psychoanalysis of Adam R. Tzaddik* (SummerWorks festival prize, 1998), *Mysterium Tremendum* and *The Offering* (nominated for a Dora Award, 2000). *Easy Lenny Lazmon and the Great Western Ascension* was nominated for a Chalmers Award, and won four Dora Awards, including outstanding new play (1998-1999).

photo by Tim Leyes

Acknowledgements

Chris Abraham's insightful direction and dramatugy greatly helped in shaping this play.

Thanks also to actors who participated in the workshops and production: David Ferry, Valerie Buhagiar, Jordan Pettle, Christine Brubaker, Jeff Clarke, Allegra Fulton, Kristen Thompson, Alon Nashman, Liisa Repo-Martell, Jennifer Morehouse and David Fox. Thanks to Elliot Wolfson, Jim LeFrancois, and especially, my parents and Ava.

In addition, I am indebted to ideas, stories, ancient texts, names and histories from the following books:

Kaplan, Aryeh. *Meditation and Kabbalah*. Samuel Weiser, York Beach, Maine. 1982.

Levinas, Emmanuel. *Nine Talmudic Readings*. (Trans. by Annette Aronowicz) Indiana University Press, Bloomington. 1990.

Levinas, Emmanuel. *Difficult Freedom: Essays on Judiasm*. (Trans. by Sean Hand) Johns Hopkins University Press, Baltimore. 1990.

Libo, Kenneth and Irving Howe. *We Lived There Too*. St. Martin's/Marek, New York. 1984.

Rochlin, Harriet and Fred. *Pioneer Jews: A New Life in the Far West*. Houghton Mifflin Company, Boston. 1984.

Sachar, Howard M. *A History of The Jews in America*. Vintage Books, New York. 1992.

Scholem, Gershom. *Major Trends in Jewish Mysticism*. Schocken Books, New York. 1974.

Production History

Easy Lenny Lazmon and the Great Western Ascension was produced by Moriah Productions in association with Go Chicken Go. It premiered at Toronto's Annex Theatre on October 10, 1998, with the following cast and crew:

LENNY LAZMON   Alon Nashman
JESSE JAMESON   Liisa Repo-Martell
MAYER   David Fox
SOPHIA   Jennifer Morehouse

Director: Chris Abraham
Set Design: Joanne Dente and Chris Abraham
Lighting Design: Steve Lucas and Sandra Marcroft
Costume Design: Joanne Dente
Music: John Millard
Stage Manager: Hilary Unger
Producer: Jim LeFrancois

Characters

LENNY LAZMON, 25
JESSE JAMESON, 25
MAYER, 67
SOPHIA, 63

Act I
Place: A deserted old road in the mythic West. A cactus by the side of the road.
Time: August 11, 1997.

Act II
Place: Same. Fresh blood stains stretch sideways across the road. A pair of bloody bull's horns sit in the street. There is red fruit on the cactus.
Time: August 12, 1997.

ACT 1

LENNY LAZMON enters in the centre of the road. He's decked out in full western gear: cowboy boots, cowboy hat, a linen shirt and clean jeans. He stops suddenly and nervously sniffs the air. Pause. He looks back, breaths deeply, then looks forward down the road. His hands are shaking, his breath erratic. He controls his breathing, then stands with one foot on either side of the yellow lines. Slowly, from a holster around his jeans he pulls out a gun. He puts two bullets in it, then aims down the road. Pause. He lowers the gun, then puts it back into his holster. He glances backward. He faces forward, again, and talks to two "figures" he imagines.

LENNY   What's that? Who am I? Who I am? Walking in your path?

LENNY smiles. Pause. He gets into a drawing position.

Alright, tough guy.

LENNY waits three counts, then suddenly draws and fires to the right.

Tutrosnay! Meet yer maker!

He aims to the left and fires again.

Suranah! In the face!

He lowers his gun and puts it back into his holster.

Now, y'all remember to tell your boss look out, 'cause Easy Lazmon's comin' into town.

JESSE JAMESON enters in the centre of the road. She's wearing jeans and a t-shirt and carrying a large, beat-up knapsack. She's dirty; it looks like she's been travelling for a long time.

Quick, what's today!

JESSE Monday.

LENNY I mean what day!

JESSE August 11th.

LENNY So that's the eleventh day of the eighth month in the
       one thousand, nine-hundred and ninety-seventh year
       of the modern era. Tomorrow's the big day.

JESSE Man, it's hot. I need a margarita.

       JESSE sits and fans herself.

LENNY They're coming, Jesse. I'll bet they're just ahead of
       us, now, waiting. Right on the other side of the
       mountains, up there.

       *On the side of the road, JESSE starts to unload from
       her bag a dirty sleeping bag and a can of beans.*

       What're you doing?

JESSE Unloading.

LENNY We can't stop here. There's lots more travelling time,
       today.

JESSE I'm gettin' tired.

LENNY It's just over those mountains! We've gotta go further
       tonight.

JESSE We're still a long way from the coast.

LENNY We are not stopping here, Jesse.

JESSE C'mon, relax. Have a seat!

LENNY Relax?

JESSE You know, sit, stretch your legs out.

LENNY   Tomorrow morning there's gonna be a road blocker
          standing in the middle of that highway with his six
          shooter aimed up our noses, and he's gonna demand
          why such unworthy people as ourselves are walking
          down his sacred path.

JESSE   Unworthy? You got some serious dedication, cow-
          boy, nothin' unworthy about that. No, only thing you
          need for tomorrow is some rest. C'mon, sit down.

              Pause. LENNY remains standing.

          I foresee a tension headache.

LENNY   You rested yet?

JESSE   Yeah, got eight hours of sleep just then.

LENNY   Let's go.

JESSE   Aren't you fuckin' exhausted? I mean you've gotta
          have at least a drink or something. How 'bout havin'
          some water?

LENNY   Jesse!

JESSE   You can't just not drink all day.

LENNY   How many times do I have to tell you?

JESSE   I don't wanna see you drop dead from dehydration in
          the middle of the road.

              LENNY packs up JESSE's stuff and picks up her bag.

          A hundred fuckin' degrees outside and you're plod-
          din' along all day like a fuckin' camel!

LENNY   The heat's starting to fade, now. It's easier walking.

JESSE   Yeah, well, I think it's time to call it a day.

              Pause. JESSE takes off her boots and rubs her feet.
              LENNY watches.

What, is foot pain not allowed on the Great Western Coastal Ranch?

She puts her boots back on.

Look, it's necessary that I rest for five minutes so I don't keel over and die. You could use some rest, too. Have a seat. You could tell me about these cowboy road blockers. They like that thing you're doing, huh? That "Y'all look out 'cause here comes cowboy Easy Lazmon, comin' into town!"

LENNY drops the bag.

LENNY   "Tell your boss look out!"

JESSE   Yeah, "tell your boss look out..."

LENNY   Don't mess it up.

JESSE   Alright, your boss then. Whatever. You got it down. I like it. And I'll bet they'll like it, too, these road blockers of yours.

LENNY   It's not a question of liking or disliking it.

JESSE   Kind-a strange, isn't it?

LENNY   It's a code, Jesse. It's what you have to do.

JESSE   What kind of code?

LENNY   It has to be letter perfect.

JESSE   But where's it come from? I mean, what's the big deal?

LENNY   I can't talk about it, you know that.

JESSE   I know...

LENNY   Are you rested yet? 'Cause I'm about done with this particular piece of road.

JESSE   You can't expect me to walk fifteen hours a day without knowing anything about our destination.

LENNY   I told you what you need to know.

JESSE   I gotta know something concrete about where I'm
headed. Sorry, it's the way I am.

LENNY   Jesse...

JESSE   I'm serious.

Pause. They stare each other down.

Just something. Have a seat.

LENNY paces and looks west.

LENNY   It's sacred knowledge, Jesse. I can't talk about it.

JESSE   Well, who actually lives out there?

LENNY   Inhabitants of the Great Western Coastal Ranch.

JESSE   The cowboys? The road blockers?

LENNY   Yeah.

JESSE   And what d'they do all day?

LENNY   They meditate on the mystery of the west.

JESSE   Sounds like a full-time job. (*Pause.*) So you wanna be
like them, I bet. Meditatin'. Inspirin' the impure
lives of other pilgrims with your profound insight
into the mysterious west.

LENNY   I don't know if I could do that. (*Pause.*) You know,
all of them were once regular pioneers, like myself.
Poor folks who came out west with nothing.
Abandoning past practices, antiquated laws and their
European hang-ups.

JESSE   I think you'll be one of the great ones.

LENNY   Great or not great, I just want to join them.

JESSE   Sure, I can just see it. Sittin' on your horse, lookin' at the land and... thinkin' about it. Hell, you got that meditation shit down. And me there, too. Ridin' out before sunrise, solo on my quarter-horse, roundin' up the cattle. Then comin' back home for hand-rolled smokes and fresh coffee, black. Damn. Havin' breakfast all together in one of those big lodges with a fireplace and the big tables. Bunch-a cowboys, talkin' cowboy talk. "Storms a-comin', Freddie." "Soupy grounds today, John." "Old Celia's got the hoof and mouth disease, god-damn-it-all-to-hell!"

LENNY   Wishful thinking, Jesse.

JESSE   Yeah, sounds too good to be true.

LENNY   I'd be lucky to get us past the road blockers.

JESSE   I imagine they're tough to pass. I mean, you don't keep your gun loaded for nothing.

LENNY   They don't look so kindly on eastern intruders.

JESSE   Like what do they do?

LENNY   They run you through the ringer, all sorts of secret tests.

JESSE   So how do you beat 'em?

LENNY   You know I can't talk about that.

JESSE   Well, you can't just leave me hangin'!

LENNY   C'mon, Jesse, let's keep moving.

JESSE   Aw, Jesus, Lenny, I'm really tired, here...

LENNY   What did you call me?

JESSE   Uh... Lenny.

LENNY   My name is Easy.

JESSE   I know.

LENNY   Easy!

JESSE   I know, I just can't call you that.

LENNY   I told you–

JESSE   I'm not callin' you–

LENNY   I told you!

JESSE   Lenny...

LENNY   Call me "Easy".

JESSE   I don't think it suits you.

LENNY   It's not a question of suiting me, it's my name.

JESSE   You're not on the ranch yet...

LENNY   Easy.

JESSE   I mean around me you can act like someone regular–

LENNY   It's my name.

JESSE   –'stead of some ultra-pious, code-recitin' gunslinger!

LENNY   It's my name.

JESSE   It's your middle name, not even.

LENNY   That's still my name, isn't it?

JESSE   "Ezekiel". Not "Easy".

LENNY   I don't want to go by "Ezekiel". That's the name of
        lost visions and long-dead prophecies. I'm in the
        future; I'm headed west.

JESSE Alright.

LENNY Thank you.

JESSE "Easy".

LENNY Without the sarcasm.

JESSE I don't think that's possible.

LENNY Easy. Just like that.

JESSE Easy.

LENNY That's right.

JESSE Easy Lenny Lazmon.

LENNY Exactly.

JESSE Well, Easy, I'm putting up camp here for the night.

LENNY Jesse, please...

JESSE I know you're eager, cowboy, but I gotta put up camp.

LENNY It's hours before sundown!

JESSE Easy does it, Easy.

  JESSE opens the can of beans. She eats them cold.

  Cheer up, we'll leave first thing in the morning. I promise. Why don't you have some beans?

LENNY I told you a thousand times, I can't eat yet.

JESSE You've gotta eat something. That or die an ugly death.

LENNY I'll eat when I get to where I'm going.

JESSE   Six whole days and not even a bite? Not even one small, sorry-looking, piss-ant bean?

LENNY   Your temptations don't exactly help.

JESSE   Man, you're weird, Easy.

LENNY   I'm not weird.

JESSE   (*smiling*) You're really fuckin' weird.

LENNY   (*smiling*) Why is it such a historical regularity that the pious, upright and wise men are always jeered at and called lunatics?

JESSE   You can be pious, upright and wise on a full stomach.

LENNY   Not with my cowboys, you can't.

JESSE   These cowboys of yours are real fascists, if you ask me.

LENNY   They only want the pilgrim to be pure when he enters the ranch.

JESSE   How're they gonna tell one way or another if you've had a few damn beans?

LENNY   They smell the food on you. Smell it like blood on your head. Once you've eaten they know you're not a member. They know you haven't truly given up your oriental origins. Not me. I'm gonna be taken seriously. I'm gonna come in hungry and pure. All they'll smell of me is my clean flesh, my pure soul, and the smoke from my Colt.

JESSE   If you don't die first.

LENNY   I still have my strength.

JESSE   Well, one thing's sure. You've got some serious discipline.

LENNY   Only what's necessary.

JESSE   I can respect that.

LENNY   Good.

JESSE   But you're missing some damn good beans.

> *JESSE eats.*

LENNY   Hurry up and finish your dinner. We're hittin' the road when you're done.

> *Long pause. JESSE watches as LENNY stands and paces. He loads two more bullets in his gun. He's in his own world. Eventually, he faces west. He talks to himself.*

What's that? Who am I? Who I am? Walking in your path?

> *LENNY smiles. Pause. He gets into a drawing position.*

Alright, tough guy.

> *LENNY waits three counts, then suddenly draws and fires to the right.*

Adronron! Meet yer maker!

> *He aims to the left and fires again.*

Ohazna! In the face!

> *He lowers his gun and puts it back into his holster. JESSE is clutching her ears.*

Now, y'all remember to tell your boss look out, 'cause Easy Lazmon's comin' into town.

JESSE   God damn!

LENNY   Watch your mouth.

> *LENNY turns towards JESSE.*

	Let's get moving.
JESSE	We've been over this.
LENNY	If we hurry we can settle on top of that range tonight. Wait up there for the road blockers to come. Then sleep gazing out on the ranch, above a city of palms, stretching by the coastline to the western sea.
JESSE	We'll never make it.
LENNY	A Pisgah view of paradise.
JESSE	Paradise? More like suburbs. Malibu palaces. Smog in the city.
LENNY	The ranch is not the suburbs. It's still untouched by the impious, gold-loving money grubbers.
JESSE	It's California.
LENNY	We're going to the holy of holies, Jesse. A life beyond law. A land filled with people who aren't interested in scrounging the dirt for gold, or in making Hollywood movies, or any other visual lie. You about done with your beans?
JESSE	Yeah, I'm done with my damn beans.
LENNY	So, c'mon then.
JESSE	Hold your horses. I've got to load everything up again.
LENNY	Well hurry up and do it.

JESSE starts packing up, slowly.

| JESSE | A bunch of crazy cowboys keepin' themselves separate like the Amish or some U.F.O. cult. That makes me nervous. Sounds kind-a culty to me. I hope they're not talkin' love and prosperity to the public, but in the meantime chainin' a gaggle of twelve year-old girls to beds in the back room. |

LENNY	The ranch isn't some sick cult compound.
JESSE	I hope not.

JESSE continues packing.

LENNY	You don't believe me, do you?
JESSE	What?
LENNY	You don't believe the ranch exists. You think I'm living in the fairy tale world of my active imagination.
JESSE	No... I mean... I don't know. Secret codes and cowboy ranches. Sacred mysteries of the glorious coast. I've never seen anything like that. I hope you're right; I really do. I hope there's all that shit out there.
LENNY	There is.
JESSE	And you say these guys are serious, huh? I mean they're not just the same old cowboy assholes I run into everyday?
LENNY	They're encyclopedic in their knowledge. It's virtually impossible to become one of them.
JESSE	Yeah?
LENNY	You know what they expect the pilgrim to have learned?
JESSE	What?
LENNY	The entire history of the west. The rush of '49, Pike's Peak, Klondike, barbed wire fencing and cattle trains. The vital importance of the Pacific railroads. Legends of outlaws, town layouts, mining ventures, geography of the land. Tribal histories, native genocide, post-war migrant patterns, entertainment from Buffalo Bill through Sam Peckinpaw.
JESSE	Pretty bookish for a bunch of cowboys.

LENNY   Cutting the 49th parallel, Polk, the Mexican War, Republic of Texas. Also the theories and movements. Manifest Destiny, the Book of Mormon, Frederick Turner and Louis Riel. These are not ordinary people, Jesse.

JESSE   But what's life really like when you get past all their tests and get onto the ranch?

LENNY   It's paradise. You ride with them all day on horseback, in the pale shadows of the Pacific coast where glory once sat and where glory sits still.

JESSE   You know I could listen to your crazy talk all night and all day.

LENNY   It's not crazy. You just don't believe me.

JESSE   No, it's just... I just don't want you to be disappointed, that's all.

LENNY   I won't be.

     Pause. They are looking out towards the horizon.

     Finish packing. Let's go.

JESSE   Okay, okay. Just let me make my entries, first.

LENNY   No, Jesse! You can do that when we camp!

JESSE   I won't be able to see shit, then. I gotta do it when it's light.

LENNY   No! No! We're going! Now!

JESSE   I'm gonna make my entries and then we'll go right after. I promise.

     LENNY paces, frustrated. JESSE reaches into her bag and pulls out two filthy looking gloves and a clear plastic bag, filled with three pieces of bloody flesh. She puts them down and then takes a leather-bound journal, also old and worn, from her bag. Slowly, LENNY gets drawn into this ritual.

LENNY   That's a nasty habit you have, Jesse.

JESSE   Pay no attention, then.

> *JESSE puts on the gloves and opens the book. From the bag, she removes the first piece of gnarled flesh and holds it up to the light.*

LENNY   What is that?

JESSE   A heart, I think. No, liver. God, smack it hard enough and it looks like chili no matter how it started.

LENNY   It's amazing to me that you touch that.

> *Slowly but rigourously, JESSE rubs the liver into a page of her book.*

You rub road kill into your diary and yet you call me weird.

JESSE   It's just what's on the road.

> *JESSE tosses the used liver into the road. She takes off her gloves, then reaches into her bag and removes a fountain pen. She writes on the page, next to the liver stain.*

LENNY   What'd you write?

JESSE   "Mark six-ten. Liver of a small mammal. Most probably, a long-eared rabbit. Found on an under-used road somewhere southwest. Day six with the Jewish cowboy."

LENNY   The Jewish cowboy?

JESSE   Your code name. You said you're Jewish, right?

LENNY   I said I *was* Jewish. Not anymore.

JESSE   Well, I mean no offense. I'm part Mormon, myself. Utah's a Zion all its own.

> *JESSE puts her gloves back on and begins the process
> again with the second piece of flesh from the bag. She
> removes it and holds it up against the light.*

Lizard. Long dead.

LENNY   Why are you doing this?

JESSE   I don't know. Don't trust the scenery, I guess. Or
people, most of the time. This'll all fade away and
I'll be left just wanderin'. But look...

> *JESSE holds up her book and shows LENNY the blood
> stains.*

Road kill. I was there. Life was there. I saw the
remains.

> *She rubs the lizard in the book with the same diligence.
> She discards it, removes her gloves and writes next to
> her mark.*

LENNY   Let me guess. "Mark six-eleven. Lizard. Crunchy
from the sun."

> *JESSE puts her gloves back on, removes the third piece
> of flesh, and holds it up against the light.*

What's that?

JESSE   I have no idea.

> *JESSE rubs the flesh into her book, removes her gloves
> and writes next to the third mark.*

"Mark six-twelve. Life and death unknown."

LENNY   That's a nice pen.

JESSE   I stole it.

> *JESSE puts the pen back into her bag and removes a
> spray can. She shakes the can, then carefully sprays
> each of the three marks in her journal.*

LENNY   What is that stuff, anyway?

JESSE   Antiperspirant.

LENNY   You know, dead things don't sweat.

JESSE   It cuts the smell.

> *JESSE waves the book in the air, to dry it out. She puts the spray can, gloves and journal back into the bag, then closes it.*

Another day, in the books.

> *LENNY stands and walks a few feet west, in the centre of the road.*

LENNY   Great, let's go.

JESSE   Hey, you see this cactus?

> *JESSE circles the cactus. She feels its firmness, tests its quills.*

It's a real beauty, huh?

LENNY   Yeah, I saw it.

JESSE   Lots of water in these. Damn plants saved my life when I was sixteen. Two weeks in the desert, all I drank was cactus juice. Yeah, the cacti know the desert. You're always safe under one.

> *JESSE starts setting up camp.*

LENNY   What are you doing?

JESSE   What d'you say we set up camp?

LENNY   There is no way we're sleeping under that spiked monster.

JESSE   If I were you I'd be cutting myself a glass of cactus juice 'stead of bad-mouthing our amigo, here.

LENNY   You said we could leave after you finished your entries.

JESSE   I know. But don't you want to rest, Easy? We can hang out, talk. Maybe make a fire. You can tell me more about the ranch. Then we'll hit the road, first thing in the morning. I mean, what's the rush? The ranch will still be there, even if we arrive a day later.

LENNY   They expect us tomorrow.

JESSE   Can't they wait?

LENNY   You don't understand, Jesse. Bad things will happen if we're too lackadaisical. Bad things like you wouldn't believe.

JESSE   Like what?

LENNY   You know I can't talk about it.

JESSE   You can't talk about anything. So how am I supposed to believe you?

LENNY   Okay. I read about one guy, an old time San Francisco-bound traveller, heading west for the gold rush, maybe 1850. He was a fraud, this guy. But after he got rich, he figured he could join up with the cowboys on undefiled ranch land. Just buy his way on. Naturally, when he saw the ranch, he was blinded by the beauty of it. The vast, shining waves on the coast. But he didn't know anything: no history, no codes, no names. Well, the road blockers have no mercy for frauds. They rode up behind him, saw this would-be cowboy staring at their sacred land and just riddled a thousand bullets in his pathetic back like little steel axes. (*Pause.*) Road blockers are like smelters. They smelt out any and all bad metal. Only the purest passes.

JESSE   You seem like the real thing to me.

LENNY   The pilgrim's perfection has to be obvious. Like a
         clear marked cross in the middle of the forehead.
         (*Pause.*) Who am I kidding? I don't know enough.
         They're gonna get me.

JESSE   You know all that shit from Buffalo Bill to Sam
         Peckinpaw, below and above the 49th parallel, right?

LENNY   Everything I study is just the beginning. There's
         always more to it. I don't know the first thing about
         the secrets of their world. I can pretend, but let's face
         it, at heart, I'm still just an out-dated, old, backwards
         Jew.

JESSE   Not just any old Jew. You're Easy Lazmon, Jewish
         cowboy extraordinare. Complete with two
         six-shooters and a first-rate cowboy hat.

              LENNY smiles.

         Besides, no one knows everything. It's a myth, these
         road blockers know every single secret of the
         mysterious west. It's just a sales pitch for the ranch.
         I mean there's some truth to it, sure, but come on.

LENNY   There're gaps in my education.

JESSE   Yeah, join the club. The way I figure, if your cowboys
         are worth knowin' they'll take us in 'cause we're
         decent. That's it. 'Cause we'll protect the ranch
         along with 'em. Of course they talk big. But bottom
         line is they're probably just really smart guys in
         classic hats with the good quality chaps. Just people,
         fightin' off failure for as long as possible, like
         everyone else. We'll do fine next to 'em. You'll see.

              LENNY paces. He stops in the middle of the road,
              nervous. He looks back at JESSE. She encourages
              him. He loads two more bullets in his gun. Again, he
              drifts into his own world. Eventually, he faces west
              and talks to himself.

LENNY   What's that? Who am I? Who I am? Walking in
         your path?

Pause. He gets into a drawing position.

Alright, tough guy.

LENNY waits three counts, then suddenly draws and fires to the right.

Tzurnik! Meet yer maker!

He aims to the left and fires again.

Dahavnoron! In the face!

He lowers his gun and puts it back into his holster.

Now, y'all remember to tell your boss look out, 'cause Easy Lazmon's comin' into town.

Pause.

JESSE   You mind stoppin' that for a while?

LENNY   I can't sleep here. I told you.

JESSE starts setting up camp under the cactus. She unrolls her sleeping bag, smoothes it out on the ground.

JESSE   Look, we've got a good place to camp, right here. We can't make it as far as you want tonight. That's a fact. Sometimes, you gotta know enough to sleep under a healthy cactus when you can get one. Even if it's got spikes on the outside. What are you looking at?

LENNY   Someone's coming.

Pause. Enter SOPHIA. She's dressed in a simple, modest dress and carrying an enormous, dirty, cloth bag over her shoulder. It weighs her down. SOPHIA walks with a disfiguring limp, one of her legs doesn't work. She has burnt scars all over her face. The scars are of words, printed backwards. Her face looks as if a reverse, mirror image of a book has been branded into her skin. LENNY and JESSE stop and watch her, somewhat horrified. Slowly, she walks across stage, across the road, past LENNY and JESSE. She doesn't look up or recognize their presence in any way. She exits.

JESSE   What the hell was that?

LENNY   Looked like a lady with a limp.

JESSE   What was all that shit on her face?

LENNY   I have no idea. I just saw her coming.

From the direction SOPHIA entered, MAYER enters. He is a portly man in his sixties, dressed in a stylish, three-piece suit, circa 1900. Neither LENNY nor JESSE see him enter.

JESSE   What's she doing carrying that load across the desert?

MAYER   Laundry!

JESSE   *(startled)* Jesus!

MAYER   Excuse me. Scared you, I see.

JESSE   Yeah.

MAYER   Hello!

JESSE   Hi.

MAYER   Hello again.

JESSE   What'd you say?

MAYER   Laundry. She's going to do the laundry.

JESSE   Where?

MAYER   In the river.

LENNY   There's a river around here?

MAYER   Well, not exactly. More like a small reservoir. And truthfully, it's got a slight chemical smell to it, rather unpleasant. But we all just call it the river anyway. Sure, we do. We might be small but we sure think big!

LENNY   Oh.

JESSE   Why doesn't she go to a launder-mat?

MAYER   Good question! Don't quite know the answer, myself. Ever since the accident, well, my Sophia just hasn't been the same. Insists on doing the laundry, same hour, every day. Insists on doing it in the river. I say to her: Sophia, there are machines. The machines can do the laundry. But no, Sophia wants to go to the water. Very good, we'll go to the water. I'll carry the burden, I say. But no. Sophia wants to carry it, as well. She insists. I apologize for her behavior; she's not much one for talking with strangers anymore. She used to be the liveliest sort. Oh, yes, sure. Hours and hours she'd make all sorts of jokes about any old thing. She knew bundles of information, Sophia did. I'm afraid now, as you see, when it's time to go to the river, she's got her purpose. Won't even tilt her head 'hello'. I'm Mayer.

JESSE   Excuse me?

MAYER   Mayer. My name is Mayer.

JESSE   Mayer?

MAYER   Sure, sure.

JESSE   I like that.

MAYER   (*loud*) The mayor!

JESSE   What?

MAYER   Mayer the mayor! Name and occupation. Well, I'm the town mayor, but I'm also a cattle herder. I raise beef cows.

JESSE   No shit.

MAYER   Oh, plenty of it.

                JESSE chuckles, half.

                Sure. My wife and I have a ranch over the ridge, on
                the other side of town.

JESSE   There's a town around here?

MAYER   Sure, sure. A town just over the ridge. Mine. Small
                town, some say it's not even a town. A stop they call
                it. A stop. That's sure the truth. Stopped me there
                for thirty-six years so far!

JESSE   (*trying to spot it*) Must be a small town.

MAYER   Oh, yes. It is. Intimate. Everyone knows every-
                body's business. Who's tittled around with whose
                wife. Whose boy came back into town looking hag-
                gard and unemployed. Which cattle have anthrax.

JESSE   Yeah, small towns...

MAYER   They knew my business, that's for sure. When
                Sophia and I married, the town paper toyed with the
                idea of printing a headline reading: "Mayer Marries!"
                That was our old editor, Reilly. Up to his old tricks.
                I think he always fancied himself a poet, old Brian
                Reilly. Imagine the headline had he known I was to
                be town mayor, someday. "Mayor Mayer Marries!"

                MAYER laughs, jovial.

JESSE   Mayor Mayer.

MAYER   Sure.

JESSE   That's cute. I like that.

MAYER   Not bad for a boy from Philadelphia, is it? Mayor of
                a small western stop?

JESSE   You're from Philly?

MAYER   Oh, sure. Philadelphia, New York. My father had us
         moving around a bit as a boy. Smart man, my father.
         He was a rabbi. Great rabbi. Gershom was his name.
         And he named me Mayer after a fellow rabbi. Also a
         smart man. So smart his name was Rabbi Wise!

         MAYER laughs, jovial. He turns to LENNY.

         And what's your name?

LENNY   Me?

MAYER   Yes.

LENNY   Easy.

MAYER   I'm sorry... how's that?

JESSE   His real name's Lenny Lazmon. He's from Montreal.

LENNY   My name's Easy!

JESSE   And I'm Jesse Jameson, sort of like the outlaw.

MAYER   Nice to meet you both. Easy Lenny, is it?

LENNY   Just Easy.

MAYER   That's a nice name, son.

LENNY   I'm not your son.

JESSE   Hey, show a little respect.

MAYER   Oh, that's alright. Young people today have new
         ways of talking and that's fine. Change. Time's
         change. Besides, Easy Lenny is quite right, he's not
         my son.

JESSE   Still, he's no business talking to you like that, mayor.

MAYER   Mayer.

JESSE   Mayor Mayer, I mean.

MAYER   Can't say I blame you, Easy. When I was a boy, my
            father made me work for a man selling dry goods,
            together with his son.... Oh, what were their
            names?.... Simon! Yes, Simon Gratz and his father,
            Michael. I hated them both. But that's right, the
            Gratzes were members of Mikveh Israel where father
            presided. Wish I could've spoken to them as you
            would've but we just weren't allowed to speak to our
            elders that way back then, even if they were bastards.
            And what a store they owned! Ugh! Dingy little dust
            box on the second floor of some run-down building
            on Market Street. That Mister Gratz had me lugging
            all sorts of old stuff up into the attic and down again.

JESSE   What kind of stuff did you sell?

MAYER   Oh, common dry goods. English damasks, satin,
            mantua, crimson India taffeties, velvet, sarsenet,
            calicos and cotton and hose, breeches, waistcoats,
            caps and garters.

JESSE   Wow.

MAYER   Also, ivory and bond handled knives and forks and
            pins and those Whitechapel needles, bombazine,
            fustian, thickset, gauze, all sorts of coloured
            calimanicoes and coloured durants and tammies,
            honeycomb shag, sure. We had also shaloons and
            buckram and nun's thread and bobbin and
            nonsopretties and camblets and Russia dowlas and
            sheeting and ozenbrigs and pewter and handsaws.

JESSE   Right.

MAYER   The usual banalities. I couldn't wait to get out of that
            shop, get out of Philadelphia altogether, and just get
            on the road.

LENNY   Speaking of getting on the road.... Sorry mister
            Mayer the mayor, whatever your name is, we gotta
            head out.

MAYER   Where you headed?

LENNY   West.

MAYER   West!

JESSE   You know, we're in no big rush, Easy...

MAYER   Go west young man! Heh, heh, sure. Heard that before.

LENNY   Pack up, Jesse.

MAYER   Where exactly are you going? Los Angeles?

LENNY   No.

MAYER   San Francisco?

LENNY   No.

MAYER   Well.

LENNY   No ordinary place.

MAYER   An extraordinary place, then. Near the sea, or in the mountains?

LENNY   Both in the mountains and near the coa. It's kind a like an old-time cowboy ranch.

MAYER   You know Sophia and I have a ranch right here.

LENNY   That so?

MAYER   We've horses and cattle, sure. And land as far as the eye can see.

LENNY   Well that's real nice for you and wife.

MAYER   You can ride all day like an old-time cowboy, right here.

JESSE   Yeah?

MAYER	Sure, sure. Perhaps the two of you would like to see it. Perhaps stay for a night or two. I could put the two of you each on a fine quarter-horse. Then we could ride out at sunrise and round up the grazing cattle. We have a guest room.
JESSE	Wow!
LENNY	Thanks...
JESSE	We'd love to! That sounds amazing!
LENNY	...but I think we have to be going.
JESSE	Lenny!
LENNY	Easy!
JESSE	Can I talk to you?
LENNY	You can talk to me on the road.
MAYER	What's the rush? Meeting family out there, are you?
LENNY	No, I don't have much family, anymore.
MAYER	Really! That's too bad. Just want to get out west, do you?
LENNY	That's right.
MAYER	Sounds like me when I was your age.
LENNY	Uh-huh.
JESSE	When'd you come out here?
LENNY	Jesse...
JESSE	A long time ago?
MAYER	Sure, sure. Thirty-six years in this little western stop. Before that I was on the road for, oh... I'd say almost ten years!

JESSE   Wow. Where'd you travel?

MAYER   Everywhere. Eventually here. But when I first left Philadelphia I made my way down to Charleston, South Carolina.

JESSE   Never been there.

MAYER   Oh, a gorgeous city. Even more so back then. Sure. You ever been to Charleston, Easy?

LENNY   No.

MAYER   Used to be lots of culture there. Things you'd like, I'll bet. Theatres, high class people.

LENNY   That so.

MAYER   I saw a play when I first got there. "Alexander Severus". Not so good. But I did meet the author afterwards and he sure was a nice enough sort. Also he was Jewish, you see. Like me. You Jewish?

JESSE   Me? No, sir. Part debunked Mormon, part Anglican. And maybe a tiny bit Navaho.

MAYER   And Easy?

LENNY   What?

MAYER   I was just wondering if you were Jewish.

LENNY   Not anymore.

MAYER   What does that mean?

LENNY   My parents were.

MAYER   Were they? I see.... I'll bet you would have liked that playwright friend of mine, Easy. Down in Charleston. Mr. Harby. He had revolutionary ideas about Jews for my day. Whole different beliefs, American beliefs. A real west coast man, he was. Only he lived on the east coast instead.

LENNY   Then that's not a real west coast man, now, is it?

MAYER   Lots of Jews, back then. In Charleston. Sure, lots.

LENNY   Well, I've lost my interest in decaying religions...

MAYER   When I left Charleston, I headed up north again to Cincinnati, where I heard a decent Jewish community lived.

LENNY   Oh God...

MAYER   Been there, have you?

LENNY   Cincinnati? Yeah. A bullshit manufacturing town.

MAYER   Well, I suppose that's true enough. The old "Queen City" has seen some rough days. But a man's gotta make a living, Easy. Sure, sure. Be it clothing, manufacturing, what have you. Now when I was there I was just visiting my father's friend, Isaac Mayer, the rabbi. My namesake. A German fellow. We had long talks about America, him and I. Sure. Boy, was he despondent. Said America's nothing but a sprawling market place, buying and selling, cheating or being cheat. And most new immigrants in America, why they'll forego intellectual pursuits, culture, all religious feeling. Because all is secondary to the riches, pure and simple. Thus, the work horse is the idol of America, the god of Cincinnati. So he told me! Now, what do you think of that?

LENNY   Me? I agree with him.

MAYER   Yes, I thought you would. I agreed with him myself.

JESSE   So you lived in Cincinnati?

MAYER   Oh, not for long. Pretty soon I got on the road, again. Out towards Wyoming.

LENNY   Jesse, it's getting kind of late...

MAYER   I'm sorry, you're in a rush.

LENNY   I'm afraid so. But it's been nice talking to you.

MAYER   Very nice, sure.

LENNY   We've got a-ways to go still tonight.

MAYER   Just keep following the road. It'll get you to the
           coast, eventually.

LENNY   Thanks. We'll be fine.

MAYER   Nice paved road, shouldn't be any problems.

LENNY   No, I don't expect any.

MAYER   Easy enough to get out west these days. Heh heh.
           Sure. Wasn't always like that, though.

JESSE   What was it like when you came?

LENNY   *(whispering to JESSE)* Stop it!

MAYER   Strange and rugged. Came out on the railroad with a
           crazy old toothless man who kept telling me to stay
           away from Colorado. Sure. Why, I asked. He said
           once upon a time his great aunt Rebecca—I think that
           was her name—she was en route to her bridegroom
           in Denver when her wagon was overtaken and
           captured by Indians in the Colorado plains, then
           offered up as a sacrifice to their gods.

LENNY   That's an old legend. I heard that one before.

MAYER   Oh, I'm sure. But I listened to that toothless man all
           the way to Cheyenne!

JESSE   Nice town, Cheyenne.

MAYER   Yes, indeed. Good cow country. Saw my first
           glimpse of the ranch life up there. For a year or so, I
           worked for this big mister mucky-muck, city-coun-
           cilor, Henry Altman. On his farm. Sure. The Swan
           Land cattle farm or something like that. Walked
           around like a little Napoleon, that guy. But what a

gorgeous herd of pure Herefords, he had! I fell in
love.

JESSE   Why didn't you stay there?

MAYER   I was young! Wanted to see the west! Much like our
friend, Easy, here.

LENNY   I've no interest in "seeing the west".

MAYER   Oh?

LENNY   A bunch of burnt-out truck stops, bad country bands
and alcoholic football players.

MAYER   Now don't get any illusions. It's always been a harsh
culture, never was pure before being defiled, never
was an idyllic place! Denver, for example. Always a
hard city, full of 'lungers' when I first came.

JESSE   What's a lunger?

MAYER   A consumptive! Tubercular folks. I remember the
West Colfax neighbourhood, it was full of 'em. Sure,
sure. They came from all over America to Denver,
'cause the mountain air was supposed to do them
good. Or so they say.

LENNY   When was this?

MAYER   I'm sorry?

LENNY   What year are you talking about?

MAYER   Oh, I don't know. They all blend together when
you're my age. You'll see.

LENNY   How old are you, anyway?

JESSE   Easy, that's rude.

MAYER   Oh, I don't mind. Sixty-seven. Don't look a day over
sixty-five though, do I?

LENNY   And there were still lungers when you came?

MAYER   Sure. Boy, Denver was the pits. I stayed with this friendly Jewish doctor, John Elsner. He cared for all these coughing lungers, he did. I used to walk with him and a woman named Saraphine around a gigantic consumptive tent-city they set up in the Rocky foothills. Did I ever try my damnedest not to get coughed on there! Heh heh. He was also a mohel, you know, Doctor Elsner. Sure, sure. I got a big kick out of that! A Rocky Mountain mohel! Heh heh.

JESSE   A mohel?

MAYER   Does circumcisions on Jewish boys. Last thing one expects to find out in Colorado, that's for sure. Ah, Denver. Don't miss that place one bit. No, the west is hard territory.

LENNY   Just 'cause Denver was always a cess-pool doesn't mean the rest of the west always was.

MAYER   It certainly does!

LENNY   No, it was once good land. Genuine cowboy country, until all the frauds came out.

MAYER   Business men, you mean. Now I have a feeling what you call fraud, I call business.

LENNY   The cowboys I'm talking about were never business men.

MAYER   Of course they were. Business is the foundation out west, never was about anything else. Not for the cowboys, nor any of their descendants, anywhere. San Francisco, for example. There was a whole community of rich Jews when I first visited, the pinnacle of society, all of 'em part of long-standing business families. Slosses, Brandensteins, Gerstles, Greenwalds. Lilienthals, Zellerbacks, Sutros and Strausses. Real cowboy families. And you think they weren't businessmen?

LENNY   Descendants of cowboys. Not the real thing, itself.

MAYER   No sir! They were true California culture! Sure, they
were the 'real thing'. I fell in with that rich crowd for
a while when I first came into town. Even got invited
to one of their weddings. A Sloss girl was marrying a
Lilienthal boy. I kid you not. I remember sitting out
back of the Sloss mansion, flowers all over the
grounds, looking at a gold-lettered dinner menu
printed on white silk! They served an eight-course
French meal. Fancy dresses, European furniture all
over the place. I tell you they were serious with their
money. 'Cause that's what western life is all about,
making money. Every marriage had to be approved
like one of their high-stakes business deals. Then all
the men went into the family business, all the ladies
joined 'society'. Society, of course, meant shopping
for frilly clothes and gold-leafed chairs at that huge
Magnin department store downtown.

JESSE   Sounds like a nightmare.

MAYER   Not my cup of tea. But they were good people, those
families. Big time philanthropists, not like the rich
folks today, who just sit on their loot, gaining interest.

LENNY   Pioneers or not, they're not in the circle of cowboys I
admire.

MAYER   Oh, who is then?

LENNY   The independent trailblazer. Living up to the true
cowboy codes.

MAYER   Like Joshua Norton, that's who you mean. Called
himself: Norton the First, Emperor of the United
States and Protector of Mexico! A real character!
Eventually, he dropped the latter title 'cause he said
Mexico was God-forsaken land and it couldn't be
protected. Heh heh. Used to walk around San
Francisco with his two mongrel dogs, bestowing his
hand-printed currency on anyone who would take it.
Wore this big blue jacket with epaulettes. A rusty old
sword, faded leather boots and a plumed hat. Ah,

San Francisco! Don't get me wrong, Easy, I was always more partial to Joshua Norton, the independent at heart.

LENNY   Right.

JESSE   He sounds like a real type.

MAYER   Oh, he was. He sure was. Now, look what I've done! I've held you up, haven't I?

LENNY   Well, it's just time we get going...

          LENNY starts packing up JESSE's bag.

MAYER   Useless old stories from my forgotten life. I apologize.

JESSE   Don't be sorry. It's interesting. Really.

MAYER   No, no, it isn't. Not for young folks. (*Pause.*) I don't mean to push but, you know, it is getting late. Perhaps the two of you would like to stay at my ranch, just for the night?

LENNY   Thanks, but we've got a place planned for tonight.

MAYER   Of course. Like I said, this road here will eventually take you to L.A.

JESSE   Haven't been to L.A. since I was fourteen.

MAYER   Good for you! No point visiting Los Angeles!

JESSE   Why not?

MAYER   It's a no good city. Never was any good.

JESSE   How's that?

MAYER   Race riots, I mean. It's a very tense place. Always has been. Even when I visited, Los Angeles was all shook up on the wake of some riot. I spoke to this police officer I met in a small synagogue, there, a

Jewish fellow, Harris. Said twenty Chinese folks had just been killed, hung, shot, what have you. All of them good honest business men, murdered by an angry white mob who hated 'em just 'cause they were Chinese. Imagine. Apparently, these days the blacks and whites are at each others throats, so I hear in the papers. No, it always was an ugly city. Best just keep away from it.

LENNY   I plan on skirting it, altogether.

MAYER   Wise move, Easy. I knew you were a wise man.

JESSE   Then where out here is worth visiting?

MAYER   No place better than my wide cattle ranch in the middle of my small western stop!

> LENNY *picks up the bag and puts it on his shoulder.*

LENNY   I know where we're going, Jesse.

JESSE   I'm just wondering what's a nice place.

MAYER   Solomonville, Arizona. Cattle country. Beautiful town, centre of Graham county in the Gila Valley, down south Arizona. I had a Passover seder in the main hotel, there, run by Anna Solomon and her husband, I.E. Sure, I did. What a fantastic seder. Cooked by their Chinese cook, Gin Awah Quang! Heh heh. Only in America do you find matzo baked by a Chinese woman served to a predominantly Mexican crowd. And all the meat was from I.E.'s ranch, fruit from Anna's garden. Nice man, I.E. A charcoal manufacturer for Harry Lesinsky's nearby Longfellow Copper Mines. Also a part time cattle rancher. What a beautiful–

LENNY   Jesse, I'm hitting the road. I'll wait for you where I set up camp.

MAYER   You sure you wouldn't rather spend the night and have a fresh start first thing in the morning?

LENNY   I'm sure. Thanks anyway.

MAYER   We've got good comfy beds. And I could serve up a meal like you've never had before. Just had a healthy two-year heifer slaughtered for fresh meat. Kosher-style, of course. A sacrifice for us all! We can sit down together, each with our favourite cut. All eat together like one big family. Sure, sure. Oh, I'm one helluva good chef!

JESSE   Oh man, that sounds fantastic.

MAYER   It's nothing. Nothing at all.

JESSE   What do you say?

LENNY   I'm hitting the road. Now.

JESSE   But Easy...

LENNY   What.

JESSE   Well, I... I'm not leaving. Sorry, this is too good to pass up. I gotta spend the night here.

LENNY   Oh, Jesse...

JESSE   C'mon, this place sounds great. He's a real nice man.

MAYER   It's just for the night.

LENNY   May we please have some privacy please!

MAYER   Sure, sure. Excuse me.

               MAYER crosses to the other side of the road and turns his back on the couple. But he eavesdrops.

JESSE   You want to go to a ranch...

LENNY   That's not what–

JESSE   He's got a full cattle shop. Horses, barns, the works!

LENNY   That's not the point.

JESSE   It's perfect. It's paradise.

LENNY   It's not perfect! What am I gonna to do out here? Sit on some buck-toothed horse with the washed-out old mayor of some hick town who didn't even have the guts or the nerve to stay all the way west? Where am I, then? Still east of Eden, Jesse, riding around the desert with a bunch of cactuses. I don't want to live on this lousy land. I want the ranch. The one out west.

JESSE   And what if it doesn't exist?

LENNY   Only small minds say it doesn't exist.

JESSE   This is the real thing, right here.

LENNY   I don't doubt it's real. Working on his cattle ranch. So is sailing around the world. So is going back home and getting some other God-forsaken job. Be a para-legal in some awful law firm. Or just sell knick-knacks to blank-faced trolls. It's all real. But that doesn't make it right.

JESSE   Have you been listening to him? All these things he remembers. All the things his life is built upon. This ranch of his has roots. It's got more roots than any place I've ever seen.

LENNY   Yeah, but so what.

JESSE   So, come on then.

LENNY   Every weed's got roots. Every cactus. This is dry earth, here. God-forsaken land.

JESSE   There's no way you're changing your mind, is there?

LENNY   I'm sorry, Jesse. You can stay with him if you need to. But I gotta go.

> *JESSE looks over at MAYER. MAYER smiles at her and tries to catch LENNY's eye.*

I'd rather you stayed with me, of course.

JESSE You would?

LENNY Yeah. Maybe I can get us both on the real ranch out west.

JESSE It's nice out there, huh?

LENNY It's paradise.

JESSE You sure?

LENNY I promise you.

JESSE Alright, then. I'll go with you.

LENNY Great.

JESSE Just let me say a proper good-bye to this guy. I like him.

LENNY Okay.

> *JESSE goes to MAYER. LENNY stands alone.*

MAYER Well?

JESSE I'm sorry, Mayer. We really have to go.

MAYER That's too bad.

JESSE Yeah, it is. Listen, though, we might come around here again some time and I'd really like to take you up on your offer if that'd be...

MAYER Sure, sure. Easy and you are always welcome in my home.

JESSE Thanks.

LENNY, worrying, is practicing draws with his gun.

You gonna be alright out here on the road?

MAYER   Oh, sure. Absolutely.

JESSE   Is your wife gonna come back soon? She's been gone a while, now.

MAYER   Yes, soon.

MAYER takes a silver pocket watch from his waistcoat pocket. He checks the time.

She always washes the clothes for the same twenty minutes. Then hangs it to dry back home. Just another three or four minutes, now.

LENNY has loaded a couple of bullets in his gun and now stands in the road, preparing himself.

What's he doing?

JESSE   Just watch. It's somethin' else.

LENNY   What's that? Who am I? Who I am? Walking in your path?

LENNY smiles. Pause. He gets into a drawing position.

Alright, tough guy.

LENNY waits three counts, then suddenly draws and fires to the right.

Zvunal! Meet yer maker!

He aims to the left and fires again.

Marginiel! In the face!

He lowers his gun and puts it back into his holster.

Now, y'all remember to tell your boss look out, 'cause Easy Lazmon's comin' into town.

MAYER   Oh, dear...

JESSE   He just started doin' it. But he's been at it all day. Sort-a crazy, huh?

MAYER   Zvunal!

JESSE   And he keeps talking about the road blockers we're gonna come up against.

MAYER   Marginiel!

JESSE   They're these cowboys that apparently guard the ranch we're going to. Says if he plays this game here, the cowboys'll let us in.

MAYER   Cowboys?

LENNY   I don't expect either of you to understand.

MAYER   I can't believe I'm hearing these words.

JESSE   You've heard 'em before?

MAYER   Well, no, I haven't actually heard them spoken out loud, but I've seen them written. Sure. My wife Sophia used to study them. Those words. In that big project of hers before the accident.

LENNY   What project?

MAYER   I'm not really sure of all the details. Oh, I asked her about it a million times. Sure, I did. But she was very reticent.

LENNY   You don't know half of what you're talking about, do you?

MAYER   I know much less than half. Her project was a bit of a taboo subject in my house. I couldn't quite decipher it. Except it had to do with Ezekiel.

JESSE   Hey, that Easy's name! Or his middle name, I mean.

MAYER   Ezekiel and his vision of wings and wheels, angels and cherubs, sapphire seats and fiery coals.

JESSE   Wow.

MAYER   And his vision of the Merkavah, God's magnificent throne.

LENNY   (*furious*) Enough!

        All stop suddenly.

        I don't want to talk about it. I don't want another single word said on the subject, you hear me?

MAYER   Oh dear.

LENNY   We're gonna go now, Jesse. We're gonna pack up our bags and say our good-byes and just hit the road.

JESSE   Jesus...

LENNY   Right now, Jesse. I'm not going to stick around and listen to this.

MAYER   That's right, you can't listen! Sure, like Sophia! She won't talk about it, either. Those words. Passwords, she said. Not to be discussed out loud. They are very ancient and very, very dangerous. How are they dangerous, I ask. But no, Sophia doesn't answer. Doesn't really need to, I guess. You can see it on her face.

LENNY   That's enough, I said. I'm done talking about it. Good-bye, Mayer. Nice meeting you. I'll wait for you down the road, Jesse.

        LENNY starts to exit.

MAYER   Wait, Easy! I won't say another word on the topic! I promise!

> *LENNY is exiting.*

But don't you want to meet my wife?

> *LENNY pauses.*

My wife Sophia. Oh, you're going to like her. Sure, I can feel it!

> *LENNY turns and faces Mayer.*

I just wish you could see her as she was back then. Way back, before the accident. Oh, she was so much happier then! And so driven! She used to read volumes upon volumes of all sorts of books. Most voracious reader I ever met. And she retained it all. Knew something about everything. Sure, she did. Biology, physics, poetry, politics, religion. Anything you could dream of talking about she'd have something interesting to say. Oh, that was a long time ago.

JESSE   What happened?

MAYER   The accident. She stopped reading after that. Our books, they gather dust. Except for the few I still read. Sophia stopped doing anything, but the laundry. That she still does. Says it's the burden she has to bear.

JESSE   What accident? What happened?

MAYER   I don't know. Honest. It was a very strange time. She had stopped eating. Acted strange. Then she disappeared for several months and just came home one day. Her face scarred and burnt, her legs broken.

LENNY   Sophia.

MAYER   Of course she didn't talk about it with me. Kept that part of her life very private. Sure, she did. You know these passwords we're no longer talking about (and I promise I'll never bring it up again except just this once), they're Jewish. Sophia said so. I recall that very distinctly. They're a proud part of your heritage, Easy!

LENNY   I'm no longer Jewish, Mayer.

MAYER   Sure, you are!

LENNY   And I don't want to talk about it.

MAYER   You're a Jewish man, indeed! You're a fine lad!

LENNY   Look, buddy, what do you want from me?

MAYER   Want? Me? Nothing. Nothing at all. You're just such a nice young man. I like you. I like you both. Such nice young people. And Sophia and I don't get to see so many younger folks these days. In truth, I'd like nothing more than for the two of you to come back with me, if you would. Perhaps stay a while. I'll teach you to ride horses. Sure, and everything you didn't want to know about cattle diseases! Heh, heh. And we'll serve you fine family meals, too, the kind you can't get on the road.

JESSE   Sounds really great.

MAYER   Yes? How about it, son?

LENNY   I'm not your son.

MAYER   No, no.

MAYER sees SOPHIA coming.

Ah, Sophia! Perhaps, we should ask her if it's alright. I'll introduce you.

SOPHIA enters carrying the huge load of laundry and limping. All stop and stare at her. She crosses the stage, oblivious, ready to pass them all by.

Uh, Sophia. Sophia, dear.

SOPHIA stops.

Would you mind putting down the laundry, I want to ask you a question.

SOPHIA puts down the laundry.

I'd like you to meet a couple of young friends. This is Jesse... uh...

JESSE   Jameson. Jesse Jameson. Hi. Nice to meet you.

SOPHIA stairs blankly at JESSE. JESSE cautiously shakes her hand and tries not to stare at her face.

MAYER   And this fine young man is Easy Lenny Lazmon. He's Jewish.

SOPHIA turns and stares blankly at LENNY. He takes her hand.

LENNY   Just call me Easy.

LENNY peers at SOPHIA's face. His expression suddenly changes. He continues to hold her hand tightly.

JESSE   Easy... Easy! Let go her hand!

LENNY steps closer to SOPHIA. He stares at her face.

LENNY   Oh my God.

JESSE   Stop starin'! For Christ's sake!

LENNY, with his free hand, slowly reaches out and touches the scarred words on SOPHIA's face. SOPHIA breaks his grip and steps back, quietly. LENNY stands, stunned.

What the hell is your problem?

MAYER   I've invited them over for the night, Sophia, if that's alright with you. Perhaps longer, we'll see. They're travellers. Without much of a home. He has no family. That alright with you, dear?

SOPHIA doesn't respond.

Yes? I assume you'd only respond if you minded, correct?

SOPHIA doesn't respond.

Sure, sure. So you don't mind, then?

SOPHIA doesn't respond.

Well then. You don't mind! It's settled! You'll both come won't you?

JESSE   I will.

MAYER   Easy?

Pause.

JESSE   What's wrong with you?

LENNY   The names. My God, those names...

Pause.

MAYER   I know! Dinner! He needs some dinner! Sure, that's it, I bet. Then a bit of fine scotch and a good night's sleep. Heh heh. I keep a bottle behind the books for these occasions. Sure, I do. That alright with you, Easy?

LENNY stares at SOPHIA.

LENNY   One night. Then we're back on the road.

JESSE   Alright!

MAYER   One night. Very well. Perhaps we should get going, then. I'll prepare those steaks if we arrive home soon.

JESSE   Great.

MAYER   Would you like some help with the laundry, dear?

> *MAYER reaches out to grab the huge bag of laundry.*
> *SOPHIA turns sharply towards him.*

SOPHIA   AAAAHHHHHHHHHHH!

> *MAYER backs off, quickly.*

MAYER   I'm sorry, then. We'll just never mind that, then. (*Pause.*) I'll just start forward, dear, and you can follow. Alright?

> *SOPHIA stands in place.*

Yes, of course. Come on, then.

> *JESSE and MAYER exit, towards the town. SOPHIA picks up the bag of laundry. She struggles to put it on her shoulder. At the same moment, LENNY picks up JESSE's bag and struggles to put it on his shoulder. Slowly, SOPHIA begins to exit after MAYER and JESSE.*

LENNY   Hey! Hey, ma'am!

> *SOPHIA stops.*

Sophia, right? I want you to see something. Okay?

> *SOPHIA turns and faces LENNY. She's still holding the laundry. LENNY stands in the road, turning away from SOPHIA. He prepares himself. He loads bullets into his gun. He breathes a couple times.*

What's that? Who am I? Who I am? Walking in your path?

> *LENNY smiles. Pause. He gets into a drawing position.*

Alright, tough guy.

> *LENNY waits three counts, then suddenly draws and fires to the right.*

Tutrobnal! Meet yer maker!

He aims to the left and fires again.

Zachapnirnai! In the face!

He lowers his gun and puts it back into his holster.

Now, y'all remember to tell your boss look out, 'cause Easy Lazmon's comin' into town.

Pause. LENNY turns to see SOPHIA watching him.

Well? What d'you think?

SOPHIA laughs, heartily.

End of Act I

Act 2

> *JESSE enters from the 'town', looking ragged and car-*
> *rying her bag. She stops in the centre of the road, then*
> *looks in both directions.*

JESSE   Easy! (*Pause.*) Easy! (*Pause. She calls louder.*) Damn
it, Easy, where are you!

> *She sees the blood on the road.*

Oh, man.

> *JESSE approaches and touches the blood. She sniffs it,*
> *rubs her hand on her jeans. She sees the bull's bloody*
> *horns in the street, picks them up curiously, then sits*
> *with them on the side of the road. She looks them over.*
> *After a moment, she decides to take out her gloves and*
> *her journal. She puts the gloves on and opens the*
> *book. When she's about to rub the horns on the page*
> *she changes her mind. She closes the journal and*
> *throws the horns back on to the road. As she puts her*
> *book away, LENNY enters behind her. He is covered*
> *in blood and ashes. Slowly, JESSE turns around and*
> *sees him.*

Jesus Christ.

> *LENNY doesn't move.*

What the hell happened to you?

> *LENNY doesn't answer.*

Where've you been? Are you alright?
> *Pause. LENNY is quiet.*

Hello! You know, they're missin' a bull, Easy. You
wouldn't happen to know anythin' about that, would
you? Or how a set of bull's horns got put in the road,
here? Or how you got all covered in blood, either?
They're pissed off! Mayer's in a panic, searchin' for

his animal, right now. And he keeps asking me, all accusatory, where you escaped off to.

Pause. LENNY is quiet.

What'd you do with his bull?

LENNY   Shot him.

JESSE   Oh, man.... He put us up in his home... no, in his gorgeous ranch...

LENNY   I killed his bull...

JESSE   You realize that he's got no kids and a whole bunch of land he's just beggin' to give away to you?

LENNY   Killed him.

JESSE   He wants to teach you his trade...

LENNY   With these fingers.

JESSE   You gotta go back and apologize this second.

LENNY   These insufficient fingers.

JESSE   You hear me?

LENNY   I hear you.

JESSE   So, come on then.

LENNY   I can't.

JESSE   Why not?

LENNY   You go back. Tell him whatever you like.

JESSE   You gotta do it.

LENNY   Look at me! I'm unclean 'til evening!

JESSE   Go wash yourself off in that river, down there.

LENNY   It smells like chemicals.

JESSE   It's water, isn't it? It'll wash off blood.

LENNY   The only water around and it's polluted.

        JESSE stands and paces. She looks over towards the town.

JESSE   We gotta hurry. You don't want him to change his mind about you. Get yourself cleaned up and say you're sorry. He's real forgivin', I think. You just got to look more presentable, that's all.

LENNY   I don't want to look more presentable.

JESSE   Please. Do it for me. Besides, how d'you expect to enter your big old ranch lookin' like a burnt tampon?

LENNY   I'm not going to that ranch.

JESSE   What are you talking about?

LENNY   I'm worthless. Over-proud. I've got dirt under my nails and false sturdiness in my voice.

JESSE   That's not true.

LENNY   Idle words burn my tongue. I'm a worm, a maggot, a putrid dung drop–

JESSE   Hey!

LENNY   Sucking pieces of the chariot as if they were lollipops. A piece of adulterated silver, bragging of my shine. A bold gnat buzzing in the terrifying eyes of the word.

JESSE   Why are you always so damn hard on yourself?

LENNY   I'm sorry, Jesse. I can't go to the ranch.

JESSE   We don't have to go anywhere. We can just stay here.

LENNY   I'm not staying here, either.

JESSE Fine. But Mayer's gonna want his bull back. Or the man's gonna need some compensation for it, at least. You didn't really go ahead and shoot the thing, did you?

LENNY Yeah.

JESSE Well, where's the damn carcass, then? Let's at least get it back to him for the meat or hide or something.

LENNY Can't. I burnt it. See? Ashes.

JESSE It's burned.

LENNY Nothing left but the ashes.

JESSE You know, we got it good, here, Easy. For once, I've got it good. Now, he's gonna think we're a couple-a crazy psychopaths, you and I. And he sure as hell won't invite us back to his home. You really burned his favourite bull?

LENNY I had no choice. It had to be the best.

JESSE I can't believe you cold-hearted shot down a bull.

LENNY I didn't kill it with a cold heart. No... I whispered to it. I saw its face before it died. Watched it breathe and chew its cud. It was helpless, fenced in. It watched me. It looked upon my face and my fear. I said to it: "Here I stand before you. A man of ignominy and shame. Easy Lenny Lazmon, bastard in ascension." I looked it in the eyes when I shot it. Blew its brains out in the pasture. It fell with a final grunt. Then lying on the dirt, twitching and oozing last bits of life...

JESSE Aw, I don't wanna hear this...

LENNY I spoke again to it, out loud: "Here I am, ready." I said it with an iron-still voice. (*Pause.*) When I was sure it was dead I took a butcher's knife from Mayer's barn. Cut manageable-sized pieces. Dragged them down to the water and built an altar

out of stones. Must of dropped the horns, I see.
Then, by the altar, I poured its bull blood. Took that
fresh blood on my fingers. Seven times I sprinkled it
on the altar with the carcass. Then burned the bull
with bits of wood, plastic, any material I could find.
Burned its skin and fat and bone. Its brains and liver
and shit. Burned it all down to ashes. Red bull, for
my cleansing, for my sin. Then I gathered those
ashes in my cowboy hat and I dipped it into the
water. Then drew it out, full. And I put that
ash-water on myself.

JESSE   And that's it?

LENNY   That's it.

         Pause.

JESSE   Well, you're not gonna go kill any more of them, are
         ya?

LENNY   No.

JESSE   Look, Easy, you haven't done anything wrong. All
         that sin of yours, it's all in your head. What've you
         ever actually done to anyone?

LENNY   Nothing.

JESSE   Okay then! That's all that matters out here. This is
         the west coast, cowboy. You got a responsibility only
         for yourself. Well, and for me too, come to think of it.
         And I guess you've also got a responsibility to the
         people around you, like Mayer. You can't just steal
         his bull and kill it. That's his property. Another
         person's property.

LENNY   Yeah.

JESSE   Hell, if there's any sin goin' on here it's that! The sin
         of stealin' and murderin' a bull, that's what! Don't
         you think that hurts Mayer?

LENNY   Yeah.

JESSE   So he deserves an apology.

LENNY   I guess.

JESSE   Okay, so go give him one. (*Pause.*) Well?

LENNY   I can't.

JESSE   Of course you can.

LENNY   I'm not sorry I killed his bull.

JESSE   Just say it, then! It's a fuckin' formality!

LENNY   Even if I did say it, it wouldn't matter. My word means nothing.

JESSE   It means plenty to Mayer.

LENNY   It means nothing in my heart. An apology from a sinner! What good is that?

JESSE   Please, just say the damn words. You don't have to mean it.

LENNY   Sorry. Can't do that.

MAYER enters, running. He sees LENNY.

MAYER   There you are!

MAYER runs up to him.

I was so scared! Are you alright? Where'd you disappear off to?

LENNY looks at MAYER, but doesn't speak.

Hello? Can you speak? Oh dear... oh... can he speak?

JESSE   He can speak fine.

MAYER   Well he... he...

JESSE   In fact, he has somethin' important he needs to say. About what he was doin'. About your lost bull.

MAYER   Maury?

JESSE   Maury? You named your bull 'Maury'?

MAYER   Why not?

JESSE   'Maury the bull'?

MAYER   What happened to him?

JESSE   Easy'll tell you.

> *Long pause. LENNY says nothing.*

C'mon, Easy. Speak! Tell him about the bull!

MAYER   He's dead, is he? My Maury?

JESSE   Yeah.

MAYER   I can see by the look on your face. Sure. Well... that's... that's too bad. A fine bull, Maury. Good breeder. Yes, a fine bull, indeed.

JESSE   Easy killed him. And he wants to apologize, too, if he can bring himself to it.

MAYER   Yes.

JESSE   And he burned it. By the water. There's nothing left.

MAYER   I see.

JESSE   No carcass, no skin. Just the blood and ashes you see on him, now. I'm really sorry, Mayer.

MAYER   It's not your fault, is it? No... it's no one's fault.

JESSE   I'm sorry for both of us.

MAYER   What's on your mind, there?

> *LENNY stares hard at MAYER, but still says nothing.*

Why'd you kill our poor, red-leathered Maury?

JESSE   Red bull, he said. For his cleansing. For his sin.

MAYER   Sin? What kind of sin?

> *SOPHIA enters from 'town', carrying her huge load of laundry. She limps across the road.*

JESSE   He said he's worthless in the "eyes of the word".

MAYER   Oh, Sophia! Sophia, dear, we found Easy! Look, he's here, you see?

> *SOPHIA, ignoring MAYER, keeps walking.*

Sophia! Look!

> *SOPHIA exits.*

Oh dear, I suppose she's in one of her moods!

> *MAYER turns to JESSE.*

Did you say 'the word'?

JESSE   Yes, sir, I did.

MAYER   The word...

JESSE   I don't know what the fuck happened to him. What set him off and flipped him out.

MAYER   I wonder.... Did you see something, Easy? Hear something strange or peculiar? What? You had a revelation, though, didn't you?

> *LENNY glares down, without speaking.*

(*to JESSE*) Oh, I know this behaviour! It's the genuine thing! Sure, sure! How he hangs his head in
shame and sits there, guilty and broken. He's only
missing the scars on his face. Wait, please, a moment.
I think I need to get my wife.

> *MAYER rushes out after SOPHIA. JESSE, confused,
> stares at LENNY.*

LENNY   Those names... so many names...

JESSE   What names?

LENNY   Pages and pages. Vessels, containers. Shells of all
that's solid. And I thought that I... I thought I could...

JESSE   What?

> *MAYER is approaching.*

MAYER   (*off*) Come on!

LENNY   Oh, Jesse.... It hurts having such a heavy word on
your head.

JESSE   What word?

> *LENNY sinks into silence, again.*

Answer me!

> *MAYER is entering.*

MAYER   Come on, dear! That's it!

> *MAYER enters, dragging SOPHIA by the hand,
> limping. She keeps her bag of laundry with her.*

There he is!

> *SOPHIA stands still, staring at MAYER.*

Over there, Sophia! By the road!

> SOPHIA *looks over to* LENNY, *who has perked up,*
> *with his eyes fixed on her.*

(*to* JESSE) Sophia will talk to him! She understands!

> SOPHIA *stands still, her burnt face blank.*

Come on, Easy needs you!

> MAYER *turns to* JESSE.

Sophia'll get to the bottom of this, yes, sure. Won't
you, dear?

> *Pause.* SOPHIA *stands in silence.*

JESSE   No offense, Mayer, but I don't think your old lady's
got a tongue in her head.

LENNY   She speaks, alright. She's got plenty to say.

JESSE   You spoke to her?

LENNY   She knows the word.

JESSE   What word are you talking about?

LENNY   The word we're responsible for knowing. The word
that lets you in. The word that sustains for eternity.

JESSE   You mean those names you recite?

MAYER   The passwords, the unspoken. Is that what you
mean?

> *Both* LENNY *and* SOPHIA *are silent.*

JESSE   Will someone please answer the question?

> *No one answers.*

So, she speaks, huh?

MAYER   Sure. Of course.

JESSE approaches SOPHIA.

JESSE   And yet you got nothing to say. Nothing. Why?
'Cause I don't know the secret passwords? That it?
'Cause the closest I've been to Ezekiel's vision was
bad acid at age twelve? Maybe I haven't done as
much research as your dirty bag of underwear, there,
but give me some credit, lady. Now, what's a person
gotta do to get through to you, huh? Pester you?
Spit on you? Kick you in the shins? I can do that,
believe me. You just wait and see.

MAYER   Please, Jesse, she's... troubled.

JESSE   Yeah, troubled. Aren't we all troubled. I got my
troubles, too. Easy's killin' your prized bulls, makin'
you hate us, I'm sure. Then he goes and gives up the
Great Western Coastal Ranch. Just like that, so now
we got nothing. Why's that, you think? What'd you
say to make him so damn depressed? I think you
better talk, lady. And you start at the beginning,
hear? First thing you said. Don't leave a damn
thing out.

SOPHIA is quiet.

Well?

LENNY   She laughed.

MAYER   Laughed?

JESSE   Why'd you do a thing like that?

SOPHIA looks at JESSE.

SOPHIA   It was funny. (*Pause.*) It was very, very... funny.

JESSE   What was funny?

SOPHIA   "Now you all tell your boss look out. 'Cause Easy
Lazmon is comin' into town." Funny.

JESSE	Okay, good start. Go on.
SOPHIA	He's covered in blood.
MAYER	That's because he killed Maury, dear. Burned him by the water.
SOPHIA	Burned a bull.
MAYER	Not just any bull, either. Our Maury, you know.
JESSE	The red one.
SOPHIA	Red. For his sin.
JESSE	What happened after you laughed at him?
SOPHIA	I went home. He cornered me. Told me things.
JESSE	What things?
SOPHIA	Cowboy things.
JESSE	What exactly did he say?
SOPHIA	Endless names and tales and cowboy histories. Hours of talk. Testing all his runaway knowledge.
JESSE	Then what?
SOPHIA	Then I told him the truth about the word.
MAYER	Which is what?
SOPHIA	Didn't just tell him, straight away. First, the story of its acquisition.
JESSE	How you acquired the word?
SOPHIA	Yes. How it was done.
JESSE	Well?

SOPHIA In the beginning, I walked for a while. Those days and nights in the desert. Wandering alone on the road, watching the moon slowly fill up. A sliver a day. I broke down, drank juice from a cactus. The only life around. And when the moon filled up that third time I found the right mountain and climbed up it. Rather, bore up on eagles' wings. The next day I looked down upon the road leading into the western ranch, and saw the distant cowboys standing firm in the path. Looking mean. Guarding the road. I chanted the names I knew. And said to them, these road blockers: "Now y'all look out for Sophia's silver bullet." The cowboys listened, nodded, and went away. That night, the moon shined bright until the clouds came. Terrifying clouds, carrying thunder within. They brightened the barren land with shrieks and howls of light. Each blast broke the sky like a demonic horn. And in the desert valley below, the lightning alchemy struck down, mixing fire and smoke from the meat of dead cacti. I watched this dense cloud of darkness and hate descend upon me; me alone on mountain top. I was afraid. Got down on my knees. Lighting snapped and burned the rocks around. I put my face in the dirt. And in the flashes of violent fire I saw buried under mud and loose stones a tattered old book. On the cover it said in big letters: "The Cowboy Code". It was the revelation of the word.

Then the lightning quieted down, but my mountain top hovered in dark storm. I opened this book I'd found and saw pages and pages of names.

Names...

The names I knew. They names I studied inside and out and knew.

SOPHIA speaks in a strange voice. JESSE, MAYER and LENNY slowly shrink back. She seems possessed.

"Tutrosnay, Suranah, Adronron, Ohazna, Tzurnik, Dahavnoron, Zvunal, Marginiel, Tutrobnal, Zachapnirnai, Zehirrinal, Broniah."

SOPHIA returns to her normal voice.

I spoke these names aloud. They buzzed and
hummed on my lips. But there were thousands and
thousands more on the pages. Infinite names I'd
never seen.

*SOPHIA's strange voice. She builds until she is in a
glorious trance.*

"Akhterinel Nah, Ispaklaria, Yofiel, Dahaviel,
Kashriel, Gahuriel, Buthiel, Tofhiel, Dahariel,
Mathkiel, Shaviel, Tagriel, Mathpiel, Sarchiel, Arpiel,
Shaharariel, Satriel, Ragaiel, Sahiviel, Shaburiel,
Ratzutziel, Shalmiel, Sabliel, Zachzachiel, Hadariel,
Bazriel, Pachadiel, Geburathiel, Cazviel, Shekinyaiel,
Shathakiel, Araviel, Capiel, Anpiel, Techiel, Uziel,
Gatiel, Gatchiel, Saafriel, Garfiel, Gariel, Dariel,
Paltriel, Dumiel, Katzpiel, Gahgahiel, Arsbarsabiel,
Agromiel, Partziel, Machakiel, Tofriel... Katzpiel...
Katzpiel..."

SOPHIA is in an ecstatic state.

And I saw. Then tumbled through Atzilut and
Beriyah and Yetzirah and Asiyah. The earth rumbled
and the horses raced around me. Horses of darkness,
horses of deathly shadow, horses of gloom, horses of
fire, horses of blood, horses of hail, horses of iron,
horses of cloud. Hooves thundering and roaring over
my head. And I, with my eyes closed. The sky
screamed and turned purple. Teeth and bones and
blood fell from the heavens like rain, forming
puddles of flesh beside me. I was red-stained from
falling body. Bubbles boiled and rose from my brain,
popping off into sweet fruits of pardes. Mango
bubbles and pear and orange. Prickly Pear cactus
fruit bubbles. I threw up a yellow, thick vomit with
maggots. My stomach knotted in pain, coated with
the residue of klipot. My ears were ringing and I had
visions of Nogah and Chashmal.

SOPHIA comes down.

Then, all had passed. I sat alone in the storm. There
were thousands of pages in the ragged book in front
of me. Endless names of the cowboys' code. Names
I'd never seen, names unknown. Each of the millions
of written letters shined and sparkled on the page.
I looked carefully at them. And behold what was
seen! The letters were not written in ink. Each was
etched in glass. A fine glimmer, as thin as ink, etched,
these letters of glass. And so I focused hard into just
one of them, the letter 'Y'. And behold, the glass 'Y'
was a window! When I looked behind this window,
there lay minuscule words within the letter. I tried to
read the miniature writing and my heart began to
race. There were volumes of words, chapters and
books within. Volumes upon volumes within the 'Y'
alone. Not to mention the other letters. And I saw
the entire lost library of Alexandria and those of
Pergamum and Congress. Every book of Dewey D.
All the poems ever crafted and composed. In Spanish
and German, Czech and Cantonese. And magazines,
lists, play scripts and journal papers. Personal notes
from friend to friend. Encyclopedias, fictions, scien-
tific discoveries. All the histories of the world. And
the television guides from major metropolitan centres.
I looked deeper still within the window-letter, within
the Y, and saw more and more still, endless books yet
to be written, books still yet to be read.

I sat in dirt and beheld this text in my hands, both the
names I'd never seen and the names I knew but had
never really known. My face burned scarlet with fear
and shame, pressed against the secret of these pages.
And above me was the emptiness of a purple
sapphire sky. Clouds rumbled and a bolt of lightning
flashed. The lightning struck the book I held in my
hands and reflected off the letters, these letters made
of glass, and shot the bolt back hard into my face,
burning and scarring me, ruining my vision, writing
my face, and knocking me back. I fell backwards
from the voltage. I fell off the edge of the mountain.
Tumbled down the rocks and crushed my leg into
three hundred separate pieces.

That's what I told your friend. (*Pause.*) And then I said to him: "Behold the face of a failure! The scars of ignominy and shame! Pale shadows of the endless word!"

Pause.

MAYER   You never told me.

SOPHIA   It was too late. There was nothing more to say.

Pause.

MAYER   What happened to the boy?

SOPHIA   He turned white and stood up and left. Guess he didn't like my story.

MAYER   Oh dear.

SOPHIA   Guess it rubbed him the wrong way.

MAYER   And now he won't hardly speak to us.

SOPHIA   Why speak?

MAYER   Why? My God... after such an experience... I wouldn't even know where to begin! There must be so much pain! So many emotions.... Guilt or fear or I don't know! I'd listen, I would. Sure! To either of you! Probably give you both good solid advice, too. An honest person's advice. If only you'd talk to me!

SOPHIA   Nothing more to say after calling forth the word. After your blood is on your head.

SOPHIA painfully picks up her enormous load of laundry. She struggles to lift it onto her shoulder.

MAYER   And where are you going?

SOPHIA   The river.

MAYER   But we're not done talking yet, dear! He's still just sitting there in his black cloud!

SOPHIA   Laundry time.

> *SOPHIA starts to exit.*

MAYER   Sophia...

> *SOPHIA walks.*

Sophia, stop, please...

> *SOPHIA walks.*

Sophia, you stop right this instant!

> *SOPHIA stops and turns towards MAYER.*

Don't make me raise my voice! I... I need you to stay, Sophia. And I think it's time we stopped all this foolishness. I sure do. What he needs is.... What you need, Easy, is to come home, clean up a bit, and get this blood off your head. Oh.... Meant that literally, of course. Sounded poetic, that. Just come on home, have a bite to eat. I promise you'll feel better. Alright, son?

> *LENNY glares hard at MAYER.*

SOPHIA   Looks like he prefers the road.

MAYER   Our town would be better for his health.

SOPHIA   Nothing to do in town but the laundry. Or ranching, governing, housework.

MAYER   My God, Sophia. Are you really so dead to the world? (*Pause.*) You know as well as I do, dear, there comes a time in every life when you have to pull off the road. Stop in town, set up shop. I had to do it. You did it, too! It may not be as glorious as visions and codes, but our cattle ranch sure beats sitting on a beat up, old road! Because this is nowhere, Easy!

You have nothing, right here! You're in the middle of a local desert drive!

I know the lure of the highway. Sure, I do! Even this was once travelled by the fancy people in their automobiles, long before that interstate up north. But like all roads, it lost its charm. Everyone has to pull off sometime. Even the most ambitious pioneer. Even Black Jack Yvenson.

JESSE   Who's Black Jack Yvenson?

MAYER   One of the first settlers of our town. A famous pioneer. When I met him, he was an ancient man, walked with a cane. Mayor of this town once, long before me. Served on the city council, and the school board. Old Black Jack and Sophia were close friends for some years. Hours a day, they'd sit out on our front porch, watching the horizon, whispering. Sure. One time I heard a story about his past. When Black Jack Yvenson was a young man, he headed west with three of his bravest and strongest companions. West, he said, to a great ranch on the coast. These four men were well-educated, sharp, strong. The best of the best of the west. They made it to that ranch, past all the challenges of the road. Four men entered. But only one man left intact. Just Black Jack. He came out alone. His hair now white as the salt flats, his eyes filled with the flame of the land. So the story goes.

What happened to the other three? "The best of the best," Black Jack said, "but still not good enough." The first, apparently, did himself in with one shot from his Colt. Too much for him to bear. The second was tortured until he went insane. For years after, he wandered from town to town, drunk, no shoes on his feet. And the third... the other, a famous outlaw... why, they cut him down, right at his shoots. But Black Jack was left alone. Only he was strong enough to survive the ranch. And there he lived for many years. Until he decided to leave.

You hear me, son? He left. Sure! Abandoned that
glorious ranch and came back to this arid, little stop.
Why? Well, Black Jack once said to me: "An endless
ranch is like an endless road. You pass over each hill
blind and alone."

The endless word. The endless ranch. That could
never be your home, Easy, no. It's nobody's home.
Old Black Jack knew better. And Sophia, despite
what she may say, she knows better, too. Black Jack
came back here, instead, helped set up a desert town
for young travellers. For folks needing nothing more
than a break from the road. A solid home, a place to
settle down after a long and failing journey. Sure.
For people like me and Sophia. And for you, Easy.
It's not perfect land, you see. Black Jack knew that.
But it's possible to live here and to breathe.

LENNY   Liar.

MAYER   Excuse me?

LENNY   You're a liar. You never met 'Black Jack Yvenson'.

MAYER   Why... I most certainly did! I remember him!

LENNY   I read the legend of Black Jack. The story of his
         journey out west. His book doesn't say all that.

MAYER   Well, I don't know what the books say about him, I'm
         just telling you what he told me!

LENNY   What he, personally, told you?

MAYER   That's right. And Sophia, also.

LENNY   Old Black Jack Yvenson's been dead for hundreds of
         years. (*Pause.*) You never met him. It's impossible.

MAYER   But I could swear.

LENNY   How many other lies have you been telling, Mr.
         Mayor?

MAYER   None at all!

LENNY   You were out in Denver when the lungers lived in the foothills? What, in nineteen-ten? And San Francisco in the Gilded Age? The eighteen-nineties!

MAYER   I could tell you all about Denver!

LENNY   Well, then, how do you explain meeting a person like Black Jack Yvenson? No, not a person... a legend, a man who's been dead for so many hundreds of years I don't even know where to begin.

MAYER   Explain? I.... I need to explain? Why is it so impossible to believe...?

LENNY   Black Jack was dead before you were in diapers.

MAYER   The fact is, Easy, my life has been a great adventure. Sure, it has! I, too, have tales of our great west; I, too, have a pioneer ranch. And I think—I hope you forgive me this—I think because mine are living stories, yes, and mine is a living ranch, you can't accept it. Or me. I'm real and not fantasy. And you prefer your lost lore.

LENNY   Nice try, Mayer.

MAYER   You prefer lost worlds and lost visions to any living, human connection–

LENNY   You got it all wrong–

MAYER   –rabid isolation instead of a family, a home community–

LENNY   I'm not stuck in the distant past–

MAYER   Yes... you, yourself are lost–

LENNY   I'm in the future. I'm headed west.

MAYER   I am not a liar! I swear to you, as an elder–

LENNY   Bullshit.

MAYER   As... as... a parent...

LENNY   Bull-shit!

MAYER   Practically a parent...

LENNY   Sophia. Ma'am.

        SOPHIA stares blankly at LENNY.

        Where's your husband from?

        SOPHIA looks at MAYER.

MAYER   Go on, Sophia. Tell them the truth.

LENNY   Is he from Philadelphia?

MAYER   Actually, Easy, to be honest, I was born in New York. But then, if you remember, my father got the job over at Mikveh Israel in Philadelphia and well... we moved.

LENNY   Is that true?

SOPHIA   From Philadelphia? No. Mayer's from here.

MAYER   Wha...

LENNY   Where, this little town, here?

SOPHIA   Our small western stop.

MAYER   But Sophia, that's just not so! You know that's not true!

LENNY   And when your husband was a boy, did he ever work in a small dry-goods shop in Philadelphia?

MAYER   On Market Street, to be precise. For the Gratzes, Michael and Simon.

LENNY   Did he?

SOPHIA   No. He worked on his father's cattle ranch.

MAYER   Don't you remember the Gratzes, Sophia? Michael Gratz and his son, Simon. They sold dry goods. In fact, for a while there, I believe they did business with the United States Army.

SOPHIA   Yes, they did.

MAYER   Ah-ha! You do remember, after all! You see?

SOPHIA   Had a contract with the government. Sold the U.S. Army blankets and wool products. Also rifle parts, and dried food.

MAYER   Well, I don't remember exactly... something like that.

SOPHIA   Michael Gratz had a daughter. Rebecca Gratz. Tough as nails. The most beautiful woman alive.

MAYER   Why, I forgot all about her!

SOPHIA   Or at least that's what everyone said. Washington Irving, especially. He loved Rebecca Gratz.

JESSE   Washington Irving? The writer?

SOPHIA   That's who. Back in the eighteen-twenties, sometime.

JESSE   Eighteen twenty?

MAYER   Oh... oh, dear...

SOPHIA   You read about them, Mayer. The Gratz family. I did, too. *The Jews of Pennsylvania.* Published nineteen seventy-two.

MAYER   Really?

JESSE   Wait a minute... you mean... you mean to tell me all those people he met, all the things he did, none of 'em were real?

SOPHIA   Plenty real. Just from books.

JESSE   The mayor of town and you're a damned liar.

SOPHIA   Mayor?

JESSE   Oh no, you're kidding me!

SOPHIA   His father was mayor here. But Mayer's never been anything other than a kind, old, cattle raiser in the middle of a vast, southwestern desert.

JESSE   He said his father was a rabbi.

SOPHIA   No rabbis in the family for over four generations.

MAYER   Now, just you wait a minute! This is my father we're talking about! He was a rabbi, indeed!

SOPHIA   He was a small time mayor and politician.

MAYER   This is my own father, for God's sake!

SOPHIA   Yes, it is. I remember him well. A very nice man. Not a rabbi. A town mayor.

MAYER   Are you sure?

SOPHIA   Yes, I'm sure.

MAYER   Oh... dear.

JESSE   What the hell is going on here?

MAYER   I... I don't know.... I can't explain.... My wife is no liar, that much I know. But how then... I got this all from books? My whole life... stolen from books?

SOPHIA   I guess you read too much.

MAYER   But to confuse it all... the words with events... real moments with... a bunch of printed pages! Just some old text!

SOPHIA sighs.

SOPHIA   It's confusing to keep it all straight.

SOPHIA bends down to pick up her bag of laundry.

MAYER   Where are you going?

SOPHIA   I have to do the laundry. I'm late. It's long past laundry time.

MAYER   Perhaps the laundry can wait, dear. For just today.

SOPHIA   The laundry's dirty and needs to be cleaned.

MAYER   But...

SOPHIA   Now. Today. I can barely lift it, already. So much dirt, and always more encroaching.

SOPHIA struggles to pick up the laundry. She begins to exit.

LENNY   Wait!

SOPHIA pauses.

I need to talk to you.

SOPHIA   I'm late.

LENNY   I killed your bull.

SOPHIA   Yes. Maury. The good breeder.

LENNY   Your red bull. I sacrificed him on an alter. I bathed in his red-bull ashes.

SOPHIA   For your sin.

LENNY   Yes, my sin. And when I finished, I waited for a cleansing vision. Flying through the desert, in North storm wind. A vision of cowboys with arms open wide and no guns in their hands. Just peaceful road blockers in saddle, singing sweet sounds. Then guiding me back to their crystal-skied ranch with sapphire sunsets. And their bodies all mixed with horses' and buffaloes'. Their heads mixed together, part human, part animal. Hands, wings and fire. Bright as a rainbow in the clouds, on a black storm day. I looked right into the water.

Pause.

I saw only a deep void. With the stench of poison chemicals coming from within.

SOPHIA continues to exit.

Wait.

SOPHIA   I'm sorry, son.

LENNY   Wait...

SOPHIA   I really am.

LENNY   What the hell am I supposed to do next?

SOPHIA   You're filthy. Wash up.

MAYER   Perhaps, I could help you there, Sophia...

LENNY   Wash up?

MAYER   ...just to lift...

> *SOPHIA picks up her laundry and puts it on her shoulder.*

SOPHIA   No, thank you, Mayer. And it's too bad. 'Cause I can't help you, either.

> *SOPHIA limps off. Pause.*

MAYER   Easy, my boy...

LENNY   Leave me alone!

> *LENNY gets as far away from MAYER and JESSE as he can. Pause.*

MAYER   Well...

JESSE   Well...

MAYER   Now what?

JESSE   I don't know.

MAYER   I have images in my mind that I'm still convinced are real.

JESSE   You can't trust images, I guess. Only flesh and blood. That's what I say.

MAYER   Easy...

> *Pause. MAYER is looking at LENNY, who is in his own world.*

You know, sometimes I don't feel much like a human being, at all. No, I feel more like an ancient city. With layers upon layers of foundations, as if the periods and rulers have changed, each governing my life in different stages. The culture, religion and architecture radically transforming in successive conquered phases over the long course of my life. One empire erects a temple, fire and war raze it to the ground. All of the rubble and remainder piled on top of itself. Within me is a buried history, submerged. At times, when I'm alone, I picture my great ancient city with walls. Steep, heavy Crusader walls. And I think: there is so much to learn from me, just by wandering my narrow streets, exploring piles of garbage, digging the ruins within. But my walls are too steep, and they hold fierce gates, and so no one dares to enter and explore this incredible history, all my buried wealth. I have no one to inherit my city. I fear, like so many ancient towns, I will rot here in the desert, swept up and covered in sand.

JESSE   But your city, there, Mayer, it isn't real.

MAYER   Sure, sure.

JESSE   Hey, it happens in the desert. I guess you're pretty
famous for mirages out here.

MAYER   Yes. Well.

          Pause.

          I suppose I should go help my wife.

JESSE   Might as well.

MAYER   Sure, that's what I'll do. Go down to the river in the
desert's afternoon light, which I still treasure so. I'll
keep her company. As Sophia, in her way, keeps me.
We will do the laundry. And then we'll pass by this
road, on our way into town, once again.

JESSE   Yeah.

MAYER   Just as we do every day. Will I find you here when
we return?

JESSE   I don't know. I kind-a doubt it.

MAYER   Are you sure? Perhaps, you'd still like to come home
with me?

JESSE   What's there to come home to?

MAYER   A nice piece of land. Cattle. Good food.

JESSE   Thanks, Mayer. But I don't think we can.

MAYER   It's a good living. And you see... I have no one. No
one to inherit my city. It could be yours. For the two
of you.

JESSE   That's real nice of you.

MAYER   Easy has no family. And you... you're also alone.

JESSE   Yeah, but I'm tired, Mayer. You know.... Names too daunting to be read or understood. Personal histories stolen from books. Your cattle farm, there, it's really something else. I love it. And I like you, too. But I got so few things in this world I can trust, I barely know where I'm standing. So I just can't settle some place where I need to weed lies from the truth. I'll take less than I want, see. Sleep under a cactus 'stead of in a nice bed. Just so long as I'm sure where I'm sleeping.

MAYER   Alright, then.

JESSE   It's been real nice meeting you, Mayer. And you take care, you hear?

MAYER   I hear. A pleasure meeting you. And tell Easy... just tell him to remember me.

>   *MAYER exits towards the water. Pause. JESSE sits next to LENNY.*

JESSE   How you doin'?

LENNY   Hungry.

JESSE   Yeah, I'll bet you are.

LENNY   What've you got to eat?

JESSE   Let me see.

>   *JESSE opens her bag, rummages around, takes out a wilted carrot.*

Not so promisin'.

LENNY   Nope.

>   *JESSE tosses the carrot into the road. Pause. They watch it. JESSE points to the cactus.*

JESSE   Hey, look! That cactus has fruit.

JESSE goes to the cactus and picks off a red fruit.

Look at that, will ya?

LENNY   Can't be. It didn't have fruit yesterday.

JESSE   Maybe we didn't see it.

LENNY   It must've had.

JESSE   It must've been.

Pause.

Here.

LENNY takes the fruit, looks at it curiously.

LENNY   How do you eat this thing?

JESSE draws out her pocket knife, takes the fruit back and cuts it in half. She hands a half to LENNY, keeps a half for herself.

JESSE   Just eat the inside.

They eat the fruit, silently.

Well?

LENNY   That's pretty good fruit.

JESSE   For a God-forsaken land.

They sit for a while in silence, eating.

What're you thinkin' about?

LENNY   The ranch out west. Rumour has it, at the door of their main lodge they've got a couch of pure platinum, glowing like the heavens.

JESSE   Damn! That stuff's expensive!

LENNY   A cowboy sits on it. Reclining and lounging on platinum all day.

JESSE   Sounds like the good job to me.

LENNY   If you've gotten past the other road blockers, and you arrive at this cowboy on his platinum couch, he stands up and asks you, all fierce and gruff, who the hell you think you are to walk in his path.

JESSE   And what do you say to him?

LENNY   "Who am I? Who I am? Walking in your path?"

JESSE   Then what?

LENNY   You get into a drawing position and you say: "Alright, tough guy."

JESSE   And then you fire?

LENNY   That's right.

JESSE   And what do you say when you fire?

LENNY   "Zehirrinal! Meet yer maker! Broniah! In the face!"

JESSE   Then that cowboy's dead, right?

LENNY   No, ma'am. The cowboy, he's bigger than that. You're just shooting his body. But the cowboy's a legend that always lives.

JESSE   So then what?

LENNY   So I say to him: "Now open that lodge door an' tell your boss look out, 'cause Lenny Lazmon has come into town."

JESSE   And then you go into the lodge?

LENNY   That's right. All the cowboys are there. They put down their guns. Instead, they pick up guitars, and harps. Play their sad western songs, western prayers, right there before you. The room's lit only by fire, and they've good hot grub. A brotherhood of proud soldiers and ranch hands, humble guardians of the land. Everyone sits on the floor, on skins and rugs, by the fire. All even and all one.

JESSE   That sounds pretty nice. Cowboy kinship.

LENNY   I can picture myself, lying there with 'em. Shaking and shuttering with joy. Feeling unworthy to my core. And the cowboys gathered around me. Telling me not to be afraid. That I'm beloved, a true son of the land.

JESSE   You know, you can head out there still.

LENNY   God, Jesse. I want to be there. For myself. So badly.

JESSE   So go!

LENNY   I want and I want and I want. Nothing but desire. (*Pause.*) I read about one guy, a book peddler before he came out to the ranch. He had a huge collection of volumes, rare books, which he cherished more than any other possession. He had to sell them all to raise money for the trip out west. Cried every time he sold a book, for he'd never get that book back. But that's what he did, for love of the ranch. Nothing else can sanctify the name of this land.

LENNY throws his fruit into the road.

Good fruit. For a cactus.

JESSE   What do you say we get moving?

LENNY   Where do we go?

JESSE   I don't know. Let's just see what else we can find in the road.

LENNY   Alright. (*Pause.*) Let's go.

> *LENNY starts exiting, west. JESSE grabs her bag and spots the bull's horns in the road.*

JESSE   Hey, Easy, go on ahead. I'll catch up in a minute.

LENNY   Okay.

> *LENNY exits. JESSE sits down in the road, takes out her journal, gloves and pen. She puts on the gloves, picks up the bull's horns and rubs their blood in her book. She writes next to it. When she finishes writing, she reads.*

JESSE   "Mark six-thirteen. Bloody scalp of a red bull. Failed offering, down by the water. My Sabbath with the Jewish cowboy."

> *She takes off her gloves. Puts the journal, gloves and pen back into her bag. Then throws the horns back into the road. She sighs, exits.*

> *End.*